AF486179

UNEARTH YOUR POWER

RASHIKA TIWARI

To those who've felt like they were never enough for anyone, nor understood.

This one's for you.

Table
of
Contents

CONTENTS

Author's note

You are amazing. You are loved. You are worthy. You are divine. You are perfect as you are. As you embark on this journey of self-love through the pages of this book, remember that you hold within you the power to create your own destiny.

Remember that you are never alone. Even in the darkest moments, there is a spark of light within you waiting to be ignited. Trust in yourself, trust in the journey, and trust in the power of love to guide you through.

Thank you for entrusting me with a part of your journey. It is my deepest wish that this book becomes a cherished companion, inspiring you to embrace your uniqueness, pursue your passions, and live a life filled with purpose and joy.

With love and gratitude,

Rashika

Introduction

My story

For the entirety of my childhood and teenage, I've never had those real "friendships", the kind of people that you can confide in or those who have your back at all times. I was always the "outsider", the "nobody". And soon enough, at the age of 8, I found myself craving to just want to be "normal", wanting to have friends for once.

There were days where I would be made fun of for my appearance or was just outcasted for absolutely no reason. I vividly remember straight up asking people if I could be their friend or if they could include me because I was just so left out that it didn't matter anymore.

Later, the age of 11, when I shifted school. It was a completely new environment where I knew no one and hoped that my life could at the very least be better here than how it was at the previous one.

It was the first year of middle school, and I was

excited to start this new journey, with new people, at a new place. But I had no idea that this will be taking a rather bad turn and would be creating more chaos in my life.

At this new school of mine, I found myself being bullied for my appearance yet once again because I was a bit on the healthier side. I was made fun of for my looks, made fun of by the "friends" I had supposedly made and was talked about by majority of the grade.

This point of my 6th grade, I started reading books. Books became my comfort, something I found solace in. They were the ones that never judged me for being me, they never "outcasted" me rather they brought me into a whole new world of new experiences and adventures. I then spent the entirety of my next 2 years only reading books, rarely talking to people at school and keeping out of people and making friends. I felt extremely lonely but I knew that I needed to push through it because I had no other choice. I used to find myself crying to sleep every night, thinking that there was something wrong with me, and that I didn't deserve to live this life and that I was not meant for it in any way.

Then came the year 2020, the infamous hit of Covid-19. Those 2 years that I spent on my own at home, were the most peaceful years I have ever had. I didn't have any friends at school that I could talk to and neither did I have any at my locality, and being completely honest it was the best feeling ever.

I didn't have to compare myself to anybody, I was working on myself, I learned more about how to manage my emotions and myself. All I focused on, was me.

2 years later, in 2022, the year where covid restrictions were put to ease, I found myself having friends and being invited everywhere and being included into friend groups and not being judged! Such a shocker. That's the moment I realized that your appearance apparently matters a lot and people base your "likability" on it. Which I am going to prove wrong as you read further along.

That year was filled with new friendships and countless conversations, yet as it drew to a close, I realized that amidst it all, I had discovered a new version of myself.

There have been countless instances where I've questioned myself over and over, but my life is very different now. My perspective on it has completely changed.

Now looking back at what I had to go through I believe that in the end, it's only you that matters, it's only you who has to show up for yourself every single day and fight for yourself because it always was you and it is always going to be you. People are bound to come and go but you, yeah you're always going to be there with yourself.

Despite facing difficult times, those experiences have been a blessing because they taught me how to accept myself as I am, how to stand up for myself and so much more.

I'm writing this book in hopes to help you know that you are not alone and that no matter how hard life is to you, you will rise up.

Every. Single. Time.

I want you to know that you matter, and everything about you is beautiful. You have absolutely no idea how many silent cheerleaders you have hoping that you achieve everything that you're aiming for!

Be yourself

Accept yourself

Stop trying to please everyone

Don't compare yourself to others

Be the best version of yourself.

Part One:

You are a priority

"I love you, but I love me more"

is it you or me?

I longed for validation

I longed for love

just so I could finally

love myself

but what's the point

to have you if I don't have me?

Introduction

Do you care too much about people that it ends up leaving you hurt and leaves you criticizing yourself?

If the answer is yes, I want you to know the importance of loving yourself and setting boundaries.

It does not matter as to how much love you have in you to give to others, if that love is not "reciprocated" or appreciated, it is a waste of energy at your part. The longest relationship you will have in life is with yourself so don't make it a toxic one! You came here all alone and will leave all alone, so understand that it's only you in the end.

We must accept that people can change, no matter how close you are to them right now or how close your bond is, it can change in an instant. So, while having that bond with a person, you should not be too emotionally attached that you are unable to step out of that relationship at any given point of time.

You need to be able to have the courage and strength to set boundaries around yourself when required so that you are not taken advantage of. You have to have the strength to cut out those people who are belittling you or are making you feel unworthy. They restrict your growth as an individual and can be very harmful down the line.
People can be toxic at times, and relationships can turn toxic down the line as well and, it is very hard to break free from those relationships or friendships that mean so much to you and are so close to your heart. But, once you do so, will see the significant change in your life. You will then have more time to work on yourself, heal and grow all together as an individual.

Circumstances around us are always changing, so the one thing that needs to continuously evolve is ourselves. I've learned that self-love is key to overcoming distress. It becomes easier to navigate any kind of grievance when we nurture our own well-being.

Real friendships

I always felt that I was "unworthy" of love, embarrassing, stupid, ugly, weird and what not.

I always used to feel that I was worth nothing to people because clearly people didn't like me or include me in what they'd do. They would rather exclude me, make fun of me and I kept putting up with it because I had no idea what standing up for myself meant.

The biggest issue was that I let them disrespect me, I let them say whatever they'd like to me, I let them do whatever they want and that I just listened, I put up with it and didn't say a word against them.

One thing that I have learnt is that if your "friends" don't respect you and constantly criticize you, you start to believe the things they say about you. You start to think of yourself in the negative light and that consequently lowers your self – esteem. People tend to "feed" your thoughts to you by constant criticism and you end up thinking of them as your own. Most of the times, others' perceptions become our reality.

So, the simplest solution is to surround yourself with positive people, people who inspire you, people who help you grow and people who do not belittle you. When I let go of the friends I had, I started learning more about myself, I started gaining confidence in myself and had high opinions on the perspective towards life.

The friends around you should be adding more value to your life.

For example, you have an extremely important final coming up in about 2 weeks that is worth over 50 percent of your grade. There can either be two types of friends, one who invite you to parties and tell you to enjoy one more night and have fun because you have more than enough time to prepare for that exam and the other set would be of those who motivate you to study by constantly checking up on you to see your progress, they help ask you questions and you have an environment where all of you are revising for the exam to make sure that all of you give your best. Which one is the better choice?

In this world of social media and influencer culture, how many of these people are really your friends? Would they be there to help you in times of need? Will they be there when you call them at 3am and just want someone to be there with you? Unfortunately, many of your friendships would not be checking these points. Many friendships are now based on partying and gossiping rather than having that emotional connect. People quickly fade away when you're in need and that is the truth. People will not always be there for you and setting expectations for them is not doing you any good either.

If you notice your friends criticizing you, and not appreciating your successes, then those might not be the healthiest friendships to have.

You are the sum of the 5 people that you are the closest to. Do those people inspire you? Do they help you grow? Do they make you want to be the better version of yourself? Having a few positive, uplifting and encouraging friends around you are way better than having 30 criticizing, hateful and "popular" friends.

Many people that I have come across never wanted to improve on themselves, they found comfort in the dark situations they were in. They chose to remain stuck. But realizing that these people are restricting their potential significantly is required, and them doing so also affects your ability to be growing as a person. It's okay to let go of these people, it's okay to outgrow people and it's okay to want to focus on yourself. If someone seems to continuously drain you, it's okay to choose yourself over them, choose people who want to grow with you, people who are not afraid of challenges and overcoming their fears.

People pleasing

People will keep disrespecting you until you set boundaries and are serious about them. I used to let people treat me as badly as they want and would forgive them just as quickly because I didn't have the courage to stand up for myself.

I am someone who likes helping people as much as I can and it was extremely difficult for me to stop trying to make everyone happy. I used to help my friends or people around me with their problems, consoling them and doing my best to motivate them. Soon enough, as a result I became overwhelmed. My emotions started to resonate with theirs, I started going down this loophole and ended up hitting one of the lowest points in life. That's when I realized that I cannot please everyone. I am not meant to do so. I am not a "therapist" that everyone has access to and I am not the person on whom you can trauma dump on. I have my own struggles and issues to deal with, and I'm the only one who can to deal with it. I realized that I needed to prioritize myself and my needs in that moment and I have never looked back since.

Learning to distance yourself from people for your betterment is an extremely important thing. As I distanced myself from people who didn't respect my boundaries and value me as a person, my life has become so much easier. All I ask for is respect and if someone is unwilling to do that for me, that's okay. They can leave. I just do not allow people to treat me like shit anymore.

Everyone has flaws, no one is perfect. You cannot be the superhero of every person's story. It's okay to be the villain sometimes. It's okay to prioritize yourself and your mental health at the cost of being the villain.

Being there for others

On the other hand, spending time with someone who is looking for people to lift them up and help them grow can also affect you.

I learned this lesson when a friend of mine was at his lowest point after a lot of issues in his life including a breakup and multiple family issues. I used to stay up until 4 am to console him amidst this. I knew that he needed to get out of that phase and he needed to trust himself enough and have the courage to stop inflicting harm on himself.

Over the course of the next few weeks (months even), every conversation we had used to be about him "trauma dumping" on me. I kept listening to him and tried my best to motivate him but that's when I gradually started to lose all confidence that I had in myself. I started crying myself to bed because I didn't feel like myself and started to feel really down upon hearing his thoughts. His thoughts weighed heavily on me. Despite repeatedly urging him to seek professional help, he insisted on confiding only in me. I tried my hardest to support him, but after a few months, I acknowledged that he wasn't willing to help himself. Then I felt that time alone could facilitate his healing journey.

I realized that as much as I wanted to be there for him, I needed to be there for myself too. I had an extremely important exam coming up and I could not mess that up at any cost. I felt empty inside and I could not take it anymore, I had to restore myself first to restore others.

I then distanced myself from all the excess negativity so that I could focus more on my upcoming exam that could quite literally alter my life and to be able to focus a bit more on myself and heal better. I felt terrible and extremely guilty to be stepping out of that situation but I knew that in that moment, that was the best thing that I could do for myself and that I really needed it. Eventually, I learnt how to understand my emotions, and when to know when it's time to step out or when to say 'no' when I couldn't take it anymore.

Learning to say 'no' when you're not in the position to listen to the feelings of others because you yourself have had a bad day or are just not feeling up to the mark is completely okay! It's okay to not listen to someone rant, about how troublesome their life is, when you're not feeling great yourself, it's okay to take time off for yourself!

Increasing the toll on yourself is not going to take you anywhere, it will rather drain you even more emotionally.

Sometimes it's okay to help yourself. You cannot pour from an empty cup.

Negative and toxic people

Not everyone is meant to understand you for you, it's okay to move on from those people and look for better ones. You are bound to have at least one person who dislikes you, no matter how good or perfect you are.

Not everyone likes me either! (and I'm totally okay with it, you should be as well) I've had people dislike me for doing good or standing up for myself. This is mainly because people usually project their emotions onto others when they don't know how to process them. Online, this usually occurs because everyone's hiding behind screens and no one has to reveal their identity. The same people that harass online, in real life wouldn't dare to say anything similar to what they say online.

The first time I was mocked was when I was around the age of 7. I was made fun of and demeaned for my weight, for my appearance and all of the good stuff. This continued for as long as I can remember, almost half my childhood and teenage. I started believing what everyone said and they slowly started to seep into my brain as if they were my own thoughts, whereas in reality, they were being fed to me by the people around me. Often, when we don't conform to societal norms or standards—whether it's due to our weight, height, complexion, or other differences—we're labeled as misfits. These differences are often exploited by others to ridicule us and make us feel inferior.

I've had people drain my energy to the point where I wasn't able to do anything myself, and kept crying all night (yes, it does happen!).

You need to remind yourself that negativity from others is unavoidable but how you respond to it is not. We're bound to face people who dislike us, demean us, and spread hate in our lives, but choosing as to how you respond to them is what makes you different and makes you stronger.

Removing or distancing from the negative people in your life can be quite a hard task but once you do that, you will see that life has so much more to offer. You'll see yourself growing, your confidence growing, and you being your best self-overall. (it's worth it, I promise! Just do it!)

Look for the 'silent haters'. The ones who pretend to be your friend. The one who is never happy or excited for you when you tell them about something that you've accomplished or are really proud of. These haters are often those who feel jealous and threatened by your success and growth. They dislike the idea of you accomplishing something and hence instantly put you down by saying something along the lines of "oh, that's not that big" or "that's nice. Hey did you see this?". They think that your success is limiting theirs. These people exist! And, you will find them on your path later on in life. All you should do is know how to spot the right and wrong ones. The right one's will always be there, no matter what. Always remember that karma is real, and what goes around, comes right back. So you do your thing, put out all the love and kindness you have and don't react to anything that anyone says, just do your best.

"No one can hurt you without your consent"

- Eleanor Roosevelt

Part Two:

Positive Habits

"All we have to decide is what to do with the
time that is given to us."

-Gandalf, Lord of The Rings

Ups and downs

In every dawn, a fresh new start

with things dear to warm my heart

In every choice, a piece of me

a life that's lived in tranquility

Introduction

Having a positive and healthy lifestyle plays an important role in your physical and mental well-being.

Imagine, your room is a complete mess, there's clothes and food wrappers everywhere. Everything is out of order and you're rotting in your bed all day.

What does it say to you? The answer is most likely that you're too lazy, you're not feeling up to the mark, you don't want to get up and be productive because it's such a mess already and you think that cleaning all of that up is going to take forever.

Now, on the other hand, imagine that your room is completely organized, all your clothes are folded and put into their places respectively, your books are put onto the shelves neatly and you have a clean room to work in.

It shows that you are putting in effort to keep your environment clean and that you like being in a clean environment which ultimately helps you be more productive.

The state of your room usually depicts the state of your mind as your room is the one place where you spend the most of your day. For example- If we aren't feeling okay and are in a bad state of mind, we don't feel like cleaning up the place around us and makes us just want to stay in bed all day.

Studies show that people who put effort into the external environments such as their room and their physical state have a much clearer mind and are more productive than others who don't pay any attention to their external environment.

Here, we see how a significantly small habit such as keeping our room clean that most of us don't really pay much attention to can play a huge role in our mental well-being.

Habits like these, build up one after the other which slowly starts affecting how you view yourself and the world around you. Our minds possess immense power to transform our lives. One simple yet powerful practice I've adopted is looking at myself in the mirror, making eye contact, and smiling. I speak to myself, assuring myself that I love me. Starting with once a week and gradually increasing the frequency, I've noticed a positive change. Don't overthink the need to smile or laugh; these actions can boost your mood and improve your life.

Finding personal ways to stay calm and happy is crucial. During my low phases, I've discovered that helping others or appreciating their good deeds can brighten my day. This intentional act of spreading positivity reflects back on me, lifting my spirits.

It's not easy to be happy and joyful all the time, but by making the effort, we can enhance our quality of life. We must accept that everyone experiences ups and downs, and that's perfectly normal. Understanding this makes the journey to happiness more manageable.

That's the power of having positive habits and striving to have a healthy lifestyle.

Choose yourself

The most valuable asset that you'll ever invest in in your life, is you.

Choosing yourself is not isolating yourself from everyone and those fancy things like disappearing for a year and coming back stronger. Social media has made us believe that we need to be a certain way, we need to like certain things and hate on certain celebrities because everyone is doing so and if I don't do that, I am missing out on the fun right? The truth is that all of that is basically stupid shit made up by people.

Choosing you is showing up for yourself, no matter how bad your day is or how others are treating you. It is taking care of yourself and respecting yourself enough to walk out of any situation at any given point of time. It is prioritizing your mental health and your needs before catering to the needs of others and being a people pleaser.

Quite the contrary of what I said above but choosing yourself is not 'being mean to everyone because I want to protect my peace' it's rather 'listening and observing what others have to say but doing what I feel is right'.

You need to show up for yourself every single day, because that person inside of you is the only one that is going to be with you forever.

For example- we all make those to-do lists where we promise ourselves that we're going to get all of that work done by tonight, how many of us actually complete the work we set for ourselves in reality?

Barely any. We all make promises to ourselves that we never fulfill or procrastinate on. Empty promises to ourselves makes our subconscious believe that we are never going to be able to complete whatever tasks we set our mind to and hence we tend to procrastinate.

Choosing yourself is also literally not procrastinating, doing what's good for you, choosing better alternatives for yourself and completing all the work you need to get done, in time.

In the end, the longest relationship that you'll ever have in your life, is with yourself.

Surrounding yourself with positive people

Energy is contagious. Be around people who are doing better than you and who inspire you.

I cannot stress enough on how important your friend circle is and the major impact that it plays on you as an individual. Have you ever met someone who just feels off? Something just doesn't feel right? It is their energy talking to you. It is their aura telling you that they have negative energy around them and feel low themselves.

Being around positive people such as those who clap for you when you achieve something and have an optimistic perspective towards life is more likely to increase your self-esteem and self-confidence.

Having people with low energy around you such as those who constantly complain and keep going into depressive episodes which they don't want to get out of, tends to seep into you where you start resonating your emotions to be the same as theirs, no matter how good you're doing in life.

But, being positive all the time is scientifically and physically not possible. It is completely okay to have bad days and bad moods! Although, you shouldn't let that define your day or your week. People who can uplift you during your bad days are the real ones!

Look for people who strive to learn more, have an optimistic perspective on life and want to be better. They will be the ones who lift you up and will be there for you when you need them because they are the ones free of "friendship-insecurities".

Taking care of your body and mind

Taking care of your body and mind is a crucial part of living a healthy lifestyle. If you look clean and think wiser, you tend to think highly of yourself and you start to appreciate yourself even more.

Your physical appearance plays a major role into your mental health, and no, I'm not talking about looking a certain way, not at all. I'm talking about looking and feeling clean, liking what you wear and liking your physical appearance most of all.

We all criticize our body by saying stuff like 'only if I could get rid of this certain thing that's wrong in my body, would everyone like me' and 'I don't like this part, I wish I could change it'. Criticizing yourself is going to get you absolutely nowhere in life, whereas if you start accepting yourself as you are and thrive to get better from there on, people will be attracted to your behavior and aura instantly (trust me). It's not about "changing your body", it's about accepting it as is and wanting to be healthier for the sake of yourself.

Get some workout in (really helps with improving the state of mind), find a signature perfume, wash up daily, eat cleaner food (cheat days are okay, but not cheat weeks yeah?), clean your room and the environment you live in, drink upto 3-4 Litres of water each day, get a good skincare routine (extremely important, both day and night), do not forget SPF at any cost, have signature jewelry that you wear, find colors that look the best on you and dress accordingly, buy only what you need and not everything that you want.

Try implementing all of the above and you'll see a significant lift in your mood and your overall mental well-being.

Staying out of gossip and drama

We've all indulged in gossip at some point in our lives. Sometimes, we don't even realize that we're doing it. Some people enjoy the excitement and thrill of hearing rumors about others and passing it on to others with changed details to feel important.

Gossiping is in direct relation with ego; we do it to feel good about ourselves, to feel that we are at a higher position that others, and to feel that we are in control of what's going on. We feel like we need to know everything to be "relatable" or "fun". We feel like we need to be able to talk about "fun stuff" and all the drama that's going on because it's trendy and I need to know it.

People gossip about celebrities, influencers and even people in real life that they just know the names of, and to be completely honest, it does not make any sense to me. You barely even know that person, you don't know who they are within, you don't know what they're likes and dislikes are, so why do we go around talking about the lives of these celebs and influencers and people that we have no idea about how they are in real life? Why do we feel the need to judge people based on something that 2 people say about them? Gossip usually stems from hatred and feeding onto that is not doing good for anyone. You're just wasting your time and energy on things that you think make you feel relatable and superior to others, whereas on the contrary, it makes you look like an insecure person who doesn't have a life and love the idea of misery.

So, distance yourself from conversations about others or try to direct the conversation to something more meaningful. Getting into unnecessary drama reduces your attention span and makes you less productive because then all you'd want to do is know more on the tea.

I've learned to stay clear of gossip and drama at all costs, and once you do too, you'll see the world and the people much differently.

Now, if anyone wants to tell me about some drama that happened, I tell them that I'm really sorry but please not to tell me about it if it's not going to benefit me in any way. I keep an open mind and listen to other perspectives but I also do not waste my time on people who have no interest in what I have to say.

Sorting your emotions

Negative emotions – sadness, anger, guilt, envy – are completely okay to feel! Feeling emotions deeply is a part of being human, so we must not hate ourselves for it or try to suppress those emotions. Instead, we must try to get to a better and healthier emotional state than the one we're already in. Sorting your emotions is a major part of this. Understanding what you feel, why you feel that emotion and understanding the root cause of the trigger is important.

If you keep trying to suppress your emotions and you keep bottling them inside of you, it's eventually going to burst out in one way or the other.

For example, I was always the "left-out" kid in middle school and used to be the one who would sit in the corner by herself and observe the other kids having fun. I used to always tell myself that it doesn't matter if I'm by myself, there's probably something wrong with me, I'm not worthy enough or everyone just probably hates me, even though I did nothing to offend anyone. All of these feelings started to pile up inside me, I started feeling like a burden and started telling myself that I would just never find "my" people. Slowly, as I entered high-school, I started to understand that instead of targeting myself and thinking down on myself, I need to first understand why I feel that way and that I needed to solve this issue within me, because it is myself who is going to be with me for the entirety of my life.

A few steps that I recommend you use to understand and sort your emotions –

1) Recognize and understand your emotions – Acknowledge how you feel.

2) Find the root cause / Triggers – Reflect on what might have triggered those emotions. They could be either events, situations, a

conversation, interactions or even a particular person.

42

3) Accept your emotions – Accept that emotions are what make you human. It okay to feel deeply!

4) Find healthy ways to express your emotions and resolve it within yourself – Try talking to someone you trust such as a friend, your family or a therapist.

Meditation

Meditation - a practice in which an individual uses a technique - such as mindfulness, or focusing the mind on a particular object, thought, or activity to train attention and awareness, and achieve a mentally clear and emotionally calm and stable state

Meditation has been gaining a lot of attention recently, and across various fields. Although, meditation to a lot of us feels hard, time-consuming and difficult to get started with. I personally felt the same way and took a long time to actually give it a try.

I'd started meditation using the 5-minute guided meditations available online. It was very awkward at first, I used to be restless and couldn't get my mind to focus on one thing entirely. I didn't quite understand how it would

benefit me. But, as I stayed consistent, I realized that meditation isn't as quite complicated as it seems to be. Gradually, I started seeing a difference. I found myself being calm frequently and the feeling of anger lessened in me. I was more in control of my thoughts, and I felt happier and was in a way better mental state than   ever.
I still only meditate for about 10 – 15 minutes daily, but I do recommend doing it for longer if you have the time. Whenever I feel not up to the mark, or am just not in the right headspace, I put on calming meditation music and just sit there with my thoughts. This really helps regulate my feelings and helps me be more productive.

Meditation helps us in many ways such as reducing stress, improving concentration, regulate feelings, help sleep better, boosts immune system and makes you feel better about yourself overall.

Just start with a 5-minute meditation daily and you will start to see the difference in you within

30 days. Practice it whenever you get time, either early morning as you wake up, in between work breaks or before you go to sleep.

Give it a try!

Part Three:

Accepting yourself

"It is not our abilities that show what we truly are … it is our choices."

-Dumbledore, Harry Potter

A choice.

I've spent so much time

at war

with myself, I've forgotten

what peace feels like

now,

I declare

peace.

Introduction

"I wish I had the perfect body", "I wish my partner wouldn't be treating me this bad", "I wish I had the ability to sing", "I wish could I change how I look" – we all have thoughts like these on a daily basis. More often than not, we don't even realize the number of times we repeat these sentences to ourselves.

Okay, If I asked you to name all the things you love, how long would it take for you to name yourself?

This question shows us on how much we neglect self-love. We're always taught certain things by the society, the rights and wrong, but we were never taught on how to love ourselves for who we are and how to be there for ourselves when the entire world turns their back against us. So now, the question that you should ask yourself: Do you love yourself?

We're brought up and conditioned to think that we must care about others' opinions, we must let anyone feel bad, but this makes us lose ourselves sometimes. We always try to impress others, be there for others, make other people feel loved, but on the inside we're the ones who don't feel loved and important.

I am all about helping others who need it, being kind and making time for others, and being there for my people, but I also keep in mind that I need to be kind to myself as well, that instead of always trying to change who I am and trying to cater to everyone's needs, I must also give myself some space, some time to know who I am and focus on myself.

Self-acceptance is like giving yourself a warm hug, flaws and all. It's about recognizing that none of us are perfect, and that's what makes us interesting! So, take a moment to appreciate your strengths and acknowledge areas where you can grow. Remember, it's all part of the journey to becoming the best version of yourself.

When you're comfortable in your own skin, you radiate confidence. Don't let the opinions of others weigh you down; focus on being true to yourself. But self-acceptance isn't an overnight thing. It takes time and effort. So, be patient with yourself and keep striving for progress.

Your physical appearance

I believe that our physical appearance is merely a reflection of how much we respect ourselves. For example – if you live a passive lifestyle where you regularly feed yourself foods that are not doing you any good and you don't workout or don't try and put any effort into how you look, people will perceive you to be the person who doesn't care about themselves, you eventually start to self-deprecate yourself which makes you feel even guiltier for the state you're in. Whereas, if you actually want to feel good about yourself, and want to appreciate yourself, you start to put in the required work such as working out daily and developing mindful eating habits.

Now, I'm not here to tell you that you need to "look a certain way" or something along those lines, beauty standards are human-made and trying to always achieve them and looking "perfect" is not something that should be your goal. It should rather be to like who you are and how you look, regardless of your size. As I stated above, working out daily should be with the intention to wanting to feel good and making yourself a better person rather than wanting to achieve a specific look because honestly, that does more harm to your body and mind than not working out.

Social-media has now become a big part of our lives, we're constantly bombarded with images of people who have the so called "perfect body". We know that most of these images aren't real, they're edited to showcase it to the world, but we tend to fall into this trap very easily and that makes us lose confidence in ourselves.

Our bodies are not meant to stay constant throughout the years, things happen, time flies. Your body is like your personal shell, the place where you should feel the most comfortable in, but now we're all taught to hate this shell of ours and to pin point every single flaw in an attempt to "make it right". But we all have flaws, that's what makes us human!

Accepting your body as it is and working towards creating a healthy lifestyle for yourself is what matters.

Comparing with others

Comparing ourselves to others is something that seems very natural to us. Honestly, it is the main reason that we feel so terrible about ourselves and our lives.

I have compared myself to others on so many occasions, where I would crave to have the lives of others and their huge friend groups but you know what? I found out that these "glamourous" lives and huge friend groups that I want to be a part of, are completely fake. Everyone is struggling with something in their life, and most of these friends aren't even real. They all talk down on their own "friends" behind their backs.

High fashion brands makes us feel like we need to "be one of them" or we need to "fit-in".

You're not fashionable if you don't wear expensive, luxury brands, you're not relatable if you don't have own an apple device, you're not successful if you don't own a Porsche, Lamborghini or a multi-million-dollar mansion. All of this are just marketing strategies created by brands to increase their sales and engagement, but we all tend to forget that and want to be a part of the crowd.

Not every post you come across on social media shows the real story. If someone seems to be enjoying their vacation in London to the fullest on social media, you may never even know that behind the scenes, they either lost their luggage or were scammed out of a huge sum of money. Not every couple that seems to be so loving and caring towards each other is doing that well in real life, they could be having arguments day and night, but they portray themselves to look a certain way on social media. To be fair, no one really posts what's going on in their lives to the root right? You don't, and I definitely do not, so why do we make ourselves believe that all that we see on social media is the real and raw footage of a certain person's life?

Comparing our lives to those we see on social media is a complete waste of our time and energy. People only show photos that they look attractive, approachable, happy and successful in; not when they feel lonely, scared or are having a bad day.

Remember, if someone is sharing images of their successful life, you don't know what they went through to get it. There's probably a lot more backstory to all that you see online.

In the end, you should know that your competition is you. You should be better than the person you were yesterday. Your focus should be on yourself and your own life and goals. You're on your own path. Be grateful for what you have and keep working for your future.

Confidence

Confidence is a magical thing. I believe in "fake it till you make it". Nobody knows if your confidence is real or not, just fake it. Nobody cares about it as much as you think they do. Being "embarrassed" of doing something is such a myth in my opinion. Embarrassment is a made up emotion. Don't feel embarrassed. What are you embarrassed of? Of who? Of what? Embarrassed of people? Why? Nobody cares.

I'm happy being myself. I trip down the stairs, okay so what? Laugh it off! The answer that I said out loud in class was wrong, so? I'm learning, wrong answers make me understand the topic even better. I don't have a voice like nightingale while singing, it doesn't matter! I'm enjoying myself, having the time of my life while singing, nobody should have the need to judge me. And, even if they are, I am just another human trying to live life to the fullest, so I will continue to be myself regardless of what others say.

Don't be embarrassed to speak up for yourself. Say that you don't like a particular thing when you don't. Speak up if you've gotten the wrong order by mistake. Say no, when you feel uncomfortable. Voice your opinions. Nobody cares if you say no for once, they will move on with their lives.

 Take up space. Put effort into dressing up and looking cute, it's your world! Don't be afraid to be "overdressed" because that simply doesn't exist. People are just underdressed. Life is an occasion, make every moment count! Don't be afraid of attention, be unapologetically yourself.

Always strive to learn. Don't be afraid of not knowing something. It's okay. We're all learning, you can't be a know-it-all. Ask people for help, they'll be more than happy to share their knowledge with you!

You are the main character. Be authentic and humble. Be yourself and spread love. Life is like a breeze, walk through it as you enjoy each day.

59

Stop feeling sorry for yourself

You are not meant to hide yourself from people. Stop comparing yourself with others because if you constantly whine about yourself by saying things like "I'm not pretty" or "I wished I had a better body", people will perceive you to be that. If you act like you're good looking, you will be perceived as good looking. If you act like you're ugly, you will be perceived as ugly. It's literally that simple. No matter how gorgeous you are, if you don't think that of yourself, people will think of you as that.

You need to accept that life is not for the weak. Things happen, and you need to overcome it. Being grateful to be here is literally the best thing that you could do for yourself. Everyone has problems and comparing them makes it no better. You need to believe that you can better yourself and your life, and you definitely will achieve that. If you constantly feel sorry for yourself, you will never attract the good. It will prevent you from evolving and growing in life. It makes you to stop appreciate the little things in life, and eventually no one will find you attractive because no one wants to constantly hear self-loathing. You need to come to terms with the fact that it happened, and you need to focus on what you have and use that strength to build up from there.

Remind yourself that you have overcome hard situations, and that you can do it again.

Becoming selfish

62

Be selfish. Literally, just be selfish. That is the best thing that you can do for yourself. Stop thinking too much about others, when all they do is cause you pain. Stop wanting to be there for everyone. Stop always trying to please everyone. Being selfish seems like such a scary thing to do but I assure you that it literally saved my life.

Firstly, stop trying to always help others and stop trying to keep those already broken relationships. They are not worth your time, or your energy. Make sure that your cup is always full before trying to give it out to others.

Prioritize your health and your choices rather than those of others'. You don't want to go somewhere? Don't go. Just say no. Saying no to something is not the end of the world, and you do not owe anyone any explanation as to why you don't want to do a certain thing either.

Whatever you want, comes first. For an instance, I was the person who always had to reply to texts as soon as I saw them, or my mind would make me feel like a bad person for not replying. That was just me for years, and always feeling like I needed to reply or redirect my attention to the thing that someone else wanted me to do made me lose focus on what I was doing earlier. But now, I focus on what I need to get done first. I complete all the work I need to do and only reply or help others when I'm content with all that had need to be done by me. It could be a day or two, but I don't care anymore. I learnt that I didn't need to be available to everyone at all times. I needed to prioritize myself, make sure that I'm okay and healthy.

Secondly, be okay with people misunderstanding you. No one knows your life more than you. They don't know what you've been through and what you've got going on. Everyone lives and behaves differently. Not everyone has the same mindset as you, and you need to accept that. Not everyone is going to like you, and that is absolutely okay! You having a kind heart doesn't automatically make everyone around you the same. If you keep thinking that they do, you're going to end up hurting yourself (trust me, I know).

Thirdly, only allow people who add value into your life. Keep people who appreciate you, make you happy, and reciprocate the love both ways. You deserve it.

Stop doubting yourself

How many times have you prevented yourself from taking part in something just because you thought that you would not be able to make or would most probably fail in it?

You won't get everything you want from life. Yes, you read that right, you won't. I say so because I know for a fact that if I'd always gotten whatever I wanted, I would most probably not be living the life I have right now, and I would most definitely not be even 1 percent close to the person I am today. So here I am, saying that I am so glad that what I thought of, never worked out. Rejection is redirection. The best things of your life, have not even happened yet. You will never learn if you never experience heartbreak, sadness and hardships. Sometimes, you really need that bad thing to happen to make you clear on what you want from life. You still have time, it's just a bad day or a bad week, not a bad life. Sometimes, you don't get what you want because maybe that thing might completely destroy you in the future. You're just being protected, not distanced. Let life work in its ways. Whatever is meant for you, will find you. You cannot let your fears win, because that will get you nowhere but stuck in the same place for ages.

What's yours, will get to you. You need to do your best to make your life something you cherish. Focus on yourself, and the rest will all fall into place. If you lose friends, a job, a relationship, just know that it was not meant for you. People will come and go, learn to be okay with people leaving and things going in the wrong direction. Take up new opportunities, love yourself, learn how to make money, and remember that all the answers are within yourself. Unlock your potential and you'll see how much more that you're capable of.

Don't let life pass by, take control of it. It's yours. Not everything will go your way, you will come across ups and downs and that will take you to what you want eventually.

Appreciate the little things

Appreciation – a word we often take lightly – holds immense power and can work miracles. Appreciating the little things in life goes beyond receiving what we want; it means being grateful for where we are, for the food we have, the people around us, the sky, the beaches, and the mountains.

The art of noticing is something I absolutely love. Look around where you are right now and try to absorb everything. You might see your childhood toy or something you once desired but had forgotten about. These treasures often go unnoticed in our busy lives.

How many times have you complimented someone in your mind? For me, it's countless times. We often think things like, "That shirt looks great on him," or "She looks so beautiful," but rarely do we say it out loud. Everyone loves hearing compliments, so why not share them with others? Go up to someone and give that compliment. I assure you, your words will be the highlight of their day, and they will be grateful for it.

Appreciate people, things, nature, and everything you can think of because being alive and being here is a blessing. Practice gratitude daily. I've found that taking a moment each day to acknowledge the good things around me – whether it's the smile of a loved one, the warmth of the sun, or even the comfort of my favorite chair – makes a world of difference in my outlook.

Life is filled with moments of beauty and joy if we take the time to notice them. During my own journey, I've learned that gratitude can transform even the most challenging days into something more manageable. Embrace the habit of appreciation, and let it enrich your life and the lives of those around you.

Part Four:

100 Reasons Why

"I don't want to survive, I want to live!"

-Wall E

Me, always.

Longing for love to mend my heart,

Seeking from others, playing my part,

But now I stand, whole and free,

Loving myself, eternally.

1) Your parents

2) Your friends, especially that best friend

3) Delicious food

4) The feeling of laughing until your stomach hurts

5) Music that immediately gets you dancing

6) Acts of kindness

7) The satisfaction of completing your to do list

8) The joy of seeing your parents smile

9) The excitement of new beginnings

10) The smell of soil after it has rained

11) Helping someone in need

12) The feeling of the ocean breeze

13) Embracing change

14) The warm feeling of a hug

15) Finding joy in the little things

16) The joy of giving

17) The taste of your favorite drink

18) The feeling of achieving a long-term goal

19) The comfort of a good night's sleep

20) The sound of rain at your window

21) The feeling of snow on your hands

22) The feeling after a long hot shower

23) Making new friends

24) Conquering your fears

25) Seeing your siblings grow

26) Getting a tattoo

27) Eating ice cream on a burning hot day

28) Drinking hot chocolate on a freezing day

29) Seeing a pretty sunset

30) Seeing stars in the night sky

31) Traveling the world

32) Meeting new people

33) The laughter of a baby

34) Stargazing

35) Gift giving

36) Receiving gifts

37) The feeling of "I love you"

38) New clothes

39) Funny jokes

40) For the people that mean the most to you

41) The adrenaline rush of a new change

42) The feeling of being loved

43) Birthday parties!

44) Spending the day with someone you love

45) Reading as many books as you can

46) The excitement of first dates

47) Singing songs at the top of your lungs with your friends

48) Late night drives

49) Unexpected travel plans

50) Holding hands

51) Being wrapped up in a warm blanket

52) Spontaneous plans

53) Disneyland!

54) Exploring new cultures

55) To giving compliments

56) Seeing flowers bloom

57) Seeing leaves fall in autumn

58) Reading the most life altering book

59) Listening to the most relatable song ever

60) Puppy kisses

61) Cat licks

62) Dancing

63) Coffee

64) A hot shower on a cold day

65) Flying on a plane

66) Viewing art

67) Trying new recipes

68) Finding the perfect pair of jeans

69) Stuff toys!

70) Inside jokes

71) Staying in bed and sleeping a little longer

72) Trying something new

73) New haircuts

74) Charity work

75) The smell of candles

76) Poetry

77) Receiving surprises at the least expected time

78) Watching someone talk about something they are passionate about

79) The sound of splashing in puddles

80) The smell of freshly baked cookies

81) New books by your favorite authors

82) New years' fireworks

83) Family traditions

84) The warmth of sunshine on your skin

85) Compliments from strangers

86) Marshmallow and hot chocolate

87) Your comfort movies or series

88) S'mores

89) Swimming in the pool

90) The feeling of sand beneath your toes

91) Thunderstorms on a cozy night

92) Long bus/ train rides

93) Memes

94) Chocolate

95) Listening to new music artists

96) Amusement parks

97) Cherry blossom trees

98) The feeling of nostalgia

99) Flowers

And at last

100)For your future self

dreams and me.

78

I'm not perfect,

I have flaws,

But out of all that I own,

my favorite will always

be me.

at the end, memories are all I have

so why not make them all about me?

Acknowledgements

Getting around writing Unearth Your Power was a very big step for me. Putting all my experiences out for the world is a huge leap, but I am extremely happy to have done it. I couldn't have done it without the support, love and expertise of all the people around me.

Thank you to my mom, my best-friend, without whom I would have never even started with this book. You were the one who inspired me to want to write and share my experiences. You've always been there and I am so so grateful for everything.

Thank you to my dad, the person who's taught me so much. All the late-night talking sessions, car – talks and you sharing your life's pieces has made me appreciate you more than ever before. You have always believed in me and for that I am eternally grateful. I wouldn't be who I am today, if not for you.

To my brother: Thank you for always listening to my rants on stupid ideas, stuff I've done or even random 2 am thoughts. I really appreciate all that you've done for me.

Finally, I'm grateful for all of you, the ones reading. I wouldn't have been able to want to go ahead with this book without you. Thank you for making it this far and it is because of you and only you that I write this book.

About the author

Born and raised in Bangalore, India, Rashika Tiwari loves her family, books, uplifting others, and talking about mental health

Rashika has wanted to be able to speak up on how to know your worth because everyone deserves all the good on the world. She has a podcast titled "Life Untied" available for free on Spotify about life journeys, it's ups and downs, people's opinions and ideas, and self-improvement. Rashika is an avid reader or a bookworm as you call it, a girl filled with curiosity, and loves helping the ones in need. She is the kind of person who wants to make everyone feel at least 1% better than how they felt before talking to her.